Hydrangea

Cover art by Frank Navin
Cover design by Shay Culligan

ISBN: 978-1-952326-20-2

Kelsay Books
502 South 1040 East, A-119
American Fork, Utah, 84003

For my daughters, Violet and Josephine

Acknowledgments

Adelaide Anthology Awards: "Into Grace," Best poem of 2018

Adelaide: "Meditation One" and "Meditation Two"

The Aurorean: "Nantasket," "Thanks for the Rain"

Adelaide: "End of Winter", "Michigan," "Witness"

Adelaide Literary Award Anthology—Best of 2017: "Every Moment is Beautiful"

Alexandria Quarterly Magazine: "Still July"

Aries Journal for the Arts: "Michigan"

Blue Max Review: "First Snow"

Chiron Review: "Don't Wake Me Up"

Fox Chase Review: "Sparrow in the Hedge," "Winter Wife"

Underground Writer's Association: "The Meadow"

Special thanks to my friend and editor Cindy Hochman of "100 Proof" Copyediting Services.

Contents

Thanks for the Rain

Every Moment is Beautiful

Emerald Year

Hydrangea

A white hydrangea in the hands
folded just so over his paper.
His face the angle of Rimbaud; meticulous, noble, redeemed
unbruised knuckles and bone of wrist extending

like the light on the surface of non-gold.
Where in the room did love go?
Careful neckline of flesh against dark shirt:
                              coercion of the heart.

The Meadow

I found love in the red stable horse

in the meadow of darkened lavender.
Early fall brings forth the deeper red
of the rose blossoms.

In the forest looking at the pine overhead
I think of Michigan
dirt and rust smell of the creek.

We inherited the bone of archers in our ankles
running through grass
Orpheus at our backs.

His sweet kisses light the way.
A smile on his face through
branches of the willow.

His sweet kisses light our way.
His smile slowly fades
russeted pine needles cover the path.

Don't tell me about death,
my child
I don't want to hear it.

September

It's the first day of autumn
my body feels the waves of the ocean
in and out like the breath of a squirrel.

Gulls fold their wings and position their bodies
toward the sun. The wind comes off the water
they sit, averted faces all together,
until a man approaches to break their prayer.

He asks me something in Portuguese.
I do not understand him, but he keeps speaking to me.
Does he know me somehow?

In the dream of the residual wave
like a breath
like a bone
like fingertips over your arm.

I have spent the day like the sitting seagulls
my question being, how do they know to sit together
facing the same way, sitting the same way,
their heads turned at the same angle?
Is it for the sake of one?

Are they following their inner heartbeat?

Do each of us reflect the other
white breast facing forward?
Impeccable boat across the waves,
I cling to your bow.

The Leaves

There is a single coral rose in the garden,
broad and blooming will it never stop
smiling?

Doesn't it see the rain, lacking sun, and refuse of leaves?

Where is the summer? Yesterday I am pretty sure
I saw the torn wings of an owl across the highway.
This is a crime.

Green vines climb the brown fence
deeper green leaves cascade into the grass
luxuriously fat, they dip into the yard
linger in September, smiling with weight
of laughter and abundance, taking up space
in my heart, filling the room
with scent of dirt and dying leaves.

Fall from Grace

Was it about the birds?
The birds come and go with their endless raucous laughter
then everything is suddenly quiet.

Was it about their indifference?

I went to the herb garden to pick some thyme
and felt the beating heart of a cricket
within the small green leaves.

It frightened me. I let him go
but heard him all night, calling my name outside the window
under the harvest moon.

The leaves fell from the trees with such grace
at four o'clock in the side yard
it occurred to me they didn't mind dying.

Don't Wake Me Up

The clematis grows tall in the garden (Phoebus once young and strong)
frail beauty as they bend to the earth, unable to stand alone,
yellow leaves fall on the parsley and confuse me with their odor.

Early October mist vanishes into twilight and the small animals sing.

I have no cure for their heartache—
they sing of resurrection, forgiveness, and the ancient silent bow of fragile pink
flowers in the west garden near the compost heap.

I don't think I will ever forget the summer and the green,
or the small round seeds gathered on the inverse of a leaf
the smooth gray stones in the backyard

the graceful way you left me
in your wake, like the crescent waves half formed following
the small strong boat headed into the sun

into the sun.

Meditation One

Let us suppose, then, that we are dreaming, and that all these particulars—
namely, the opening of the eyes, the motion of the head, the forth-putting of
the hands—are merely illusions; and even that we really possess neither an
entire body nor hands such as we see.
                    —René Descartes, Meditations on First Philosophy

Sadness seeps in
to the corners of my brittle body.
I wake to adolescent children talking
and fall in the air.

A praying mantis came into the living room
and stared at my daughter and me;
huge soft eyes so kind
what to do about that?

It was teaching me about stillness.
It was a hard lesson.
I can't let go of summer.

Meditation Two

I lost a thread of myself in a Bill Evans song—
no matter the title
you get the picture.

Slow unraveling of smoke
decimated
like the smattering cigar ash.

When someone holds your hand,
try and remember it,
not like the rain,

feel the lines of the hand
the slow energy of their hair
between the nape of the neck and the collarbone

take in where they place their hand
the weight of the hand on your hip
notice where the hair from the scalp ends

and the neck recedes into slow movement
like a song
that leaves you transparent and lost

the road forgotten
the flowers you saw only yesterday, now brown
there is still that feeling

the recess of green in the convex nature of the leaf
that you have avoided since 11 years of age,
which is when you last saw everything as it was
on the grass looking up into the crab-apple tree.

Meditation Three

I was in the mind of the snow
I was in the mind of the squirrel

when the first light snow hits the highway
you are temporarily blinded
because the windshield is suddenly dark and white;
it is also because of your tears, which blind you
to perception, and it is as if something else—
some other voice—tells you

everything is going to be all right.

The iris of the cat expands
and decreases with wonder and interest, such is the marker of the
    body,
which informs the mind of intention and desire.

Ich liebe dich.

Winter Wife

First Snow

Should I take down the bird feeder? Or do the birds have other
plans?

A blue jay flies up
blue, black, and white feathers
connect sky, heaven, and earth;
my heart goes with it.

The moon is half silver and follows me to my car
dusk settles into low white clouds, so I perceive
the snow will fall like a heavy piece of fruit
like a woman ready to drop down into birth
the end of the beginning.

I think I will leave the bird feeders out
to be covered in the thin snow
to dangle in the small wind
with the sun shining on the plastic.

Out My Window

Out my window I hear the small black-winged song sparrow
and his brother.
In the heavy still snow gray feathers stand out.

The brown branches of the hedges are uncovered;
broken and mutilated by the storms
of January and February.

I lie in bed listening for the sparrows
only yesterday they came
2 in the window.

Outside the winter sparrows gather their friends together
they do not weep and they are not afraid.
Surely they see the ravaged hedge.
The corrupted dream of daylight
recedes into the glint of the black pupil of one eye.

Sparrow in the Hedge

Yes, I will be thy priest and build a fane
In some untrodden region of my mind
          —John Keats, "Ode to Psyche"

Each bird sings from the hedge his
sad sweet song that does not require

a backstory of time and place.
Do these sparrows somehow lift into their hearts

a past dream of young love,
or do they lift with them chance, into the billowing sky,

small beating hearts against the terrible whiteness?
Do their twig-like ankles fear the snow?

The small dark eye flits against snowflakes
the dark black beak shines in the snow branch

as the bird sings in the hedge of his lost love
his small wish, his golden youth, his boyhood,

his parents both gone. He sings of his
chance in the hedge to be redeemed

as the snowflakes slide off his speckled wing.
He endures it all with his brave little face

and his sturdy shiny eye on the endless looming
white sky in the first week of February

does he not see the thick snow on the fence,
or every branch covered in white?

Safe

Snow encases the branches of the pine
and the small trees against the highway.
Nothing moves except the snowflakes falling from the sky.

I drive my daughter to the airport to say goodbye;
nothing moves in the night.
One waits for dawn with a sort of glee.

She will not leave or grow up
she is still
11 with her feet on the dash.

The snow is heavy as to bend
the branches or to hold them completely.
Everything is quiet except

a man driving a plow truck into the night
cigarette in his mouth
safe.

Corazón (Narcissus)

I found your letter in the street and picked it up
it told me of a love like a broken winter fox sparrow sings
over the frozen puddle, staring like Narcissus into the glass
eye of nothing.

I found your letter, *Corazón,* in the snow
it told me of your summer nights and your elusive smile on her
shoulder
how you held her in your arms all night
and she let you.

I found your letter, *mi cielo,* and held it in my shaking hands
it told me about your strong young heart and your breath on her
neck.
Although she never returned your calls and slept with someone
else,
you still want her.

I put your letter in my pocket and it stirs my heart into
remorse for all those I hurt, and now I am like them;
a reflection in the eye of a small freckled bird.
I dream of you.

Cat in the Window

When my back is against your back
you outline my scapula with your fingertip.
Some people call this an angel's wing.

When you left, the snow fell against my windshield
one flake at a time, until there was an edging of thinness, barely
noticeable to the driver but necessary to remove.

I have lost touch with the birds and their concerns.

Betrayal of the Heart

Into Grace

My voice is no longer recognizable.
My fingers have betrayed me.

The way the body moves on.
An older fighter
heavy
broken
disrepaired

into grace.

I have focused on the curled brown leaves of the lawn
and even how the very next day everything has changed.

Gifts

There is a series of dead mice in the driveway
what a catastrophe!

Small brown bodies lie on their sides, tails carefully curled around
them.
I step aside

into the street   into the light   into grace.

The gray cat moves his whiskers forward
I suppose he has done this all for me.

On the computer screen
words come before movements

negative space the interbreath of our design
our lives before and after

that sweet space.

Betrayal of the Heart

I sat at the small ice-cream table I inherited
from another generation.
Wrists exposed.

You left me here alone—
to be fair, I got married;

nevertheless,
you left me here alone.

Your face is etched in my mind.
You are 22,
the perfect age for forgetting

your smile
sanguine sapphire usurped
by my small body for a small space of time.

Pleasure is never at home[*]

All things are spoiled by use.
Where is the soft-shadowed eye sleeping next to me?
Where is the hand, however strong, once against my ribs, now a
barrier?
Where is the slow beguiled smile in your aged falseness?
Where is your face I looked for everywhere?

Pleasure is never at home in the small spaces of the heart.

I create my prison string like Ariadne
to free myself,
to elevate sadness,
to imagine flight
in those careful steps I took away from you like a

shadow underneath the sleep
of your closed eye unknowing,
as I separate myself from you
into the glittering light of the kitchen window
pleasure is never at home.

---

[*] Title taken from lines in the poem "Fancy," by John Keats

Recognize me if you can

you who were made before I was unmade
        —Dante, Inferno, Canto VI

I am in the third circle of rain
and there is also snow, which barely sits
in the brown bare branches outside the bedroom window.

There is no small bird craving food
and no sound of longing;
there is only the sound of the wind

and the steel wire moving.
To let you in the door was to betray myself
to allow you to text me was a betrayal of the heart

even after lying and pretending to myself
that I enjoyed your hands on my body
like a winter bird just taking what I could.

I am not ashamed, but it is time to renegotiate
the way silence falls upon the heart at two in the morning
during a snowstorm, with the wind hailing all corners of the mind.

Death of the Robin

I shall at last be worn out and perish, like an old nutmeg-grater, grated to pieces by the constant attrition of the wood, that is, the nutmeg.
—Melville to Hawthorne, Letter, 1851

Part I

On a cold Valentine's Day
the remaining berries from the mulberry tree
fell into the snow,
scattered blue, still attached to the light branches.
It was then I realized they had been there all along
in the tree above the raised herb garden (now covered with white).

The dividends of winter are hard to bear
patches of ice and the idea that you will be left eventually
the robin sits, robust dark red against the snow.
How did he imagine his last winter in the middle of his life?

Part II

The morning crow cawed at the small sparrows;
he was not harsh, but he was relentless.

When I left the house,
I saw the robin in the tree,
his eye outlined in yellow.
He was in the branch where the dark berries held their hue;
he was very large
in point of fact, he was a king
in the branch alone mid-January
just before the bitter storm.

Part III

The robin was waiting for me in the holly bush when I came home.
Surely he could feel the storm coming.
They used to say that the robin's breast is red
because he tried to pluck the crown of thorns
from the head of Christ
and in doing so was pierced by the thorns,
the blood spread to his breast.
He is also associated with the knights,
or is that in my mind?

Part IV

It is late spring the robin has left us.
Melville writes to Hawthorne that they must "dig a deep hole"
he writes of his nag "dragging me home his winter dinner"
and I think on that—the winter dinners
are like our childhood dreams
in the mind's eye we see ourselves
as if we were looking at a picture of ourselves at five
the face unsmiling and round
holding Brother's hand.
What have we just seen?
A slap, a turtle moving across the kitchen floor,
the young cat stealing fried fish for her attic litter?

Mind how elegant men, when they talk to each other
over the garden gate, gesture.
Mind how the robin in his last days stood in the side garden
over the rugged dirt contemplating,
dragging his winter dinner forward into early spring
the mice have had their way
they too are lost at the side of the house
curled against the crumbling foundation.

Thanks for the Rain

Thanks for the Rain Part I

The white hyacinths found their way to the side garden and the
grape hyacinths mysteriously border the broken fairy, who, frankly,
could not endure the winter.

I am with her
pleasant face, fleeting skirt, show me she still has her resolve.
But for how long?

Thanks for the Rain Part II

In a dream I worked in the carwash
not pumping gas, the part where they shine the car.
Eventually, I went to buy donuts for my family.
The cashier took forever.

But then she said,
"Did you discover the beauty you never thought you had?"

So I went to the forest.

It wasn't like the birch tree was struck down
as much as it fell halfway
and stayed there
like the arc of the arm of one of Pina Bausch's dancers,
the inside muscle being the whole point

or the color of green on the underside of the leaf;
when you think all is lost
there it is,
the sun shining through
even brighter than before.

The white paper skin of the birch
falling
the small yellow leaves of the elm
falling
through the air

their grace,
listless.

Small red maple leaves
stamp the pavement
each leaf is outlined in black.

The scarlet finished lines
and the red within almost invisible.

Every Moment is Beautiful

Rose of Sharon

Feast of Immaculate Conception
Peaches with mint on a glass plate in the garden
Sun in Leo

Every Moment Is Beautiful

Every moment is beautiful
and the robin is gone.

Desire makes everything blossom
I was there when you took your hat off and shook your hair
like the blond mane of a lion.

They called you *Sam the Lion.*
I called you *sailor.*

All winter I longed for chocolate.
And now it is spring—

The crocuses have shot up,
situating themselves around the fairy.
She waves at them with her golden locks.

Your eyes are green
and your brow black.

Too soon the daylight comes
and the dream disappears
right before your eyes.

Too late, the fairy waves her hand
at the small purple and white flowers
gathered unlikely in the side yard,
where the robin once had his fill.

(Proust: "Desire makes all things blossom")

Gypsy Moths

In the garden the birds chirp
the crows caw,
a saw penetrates the air

gypsy moths have taken over and are circling the house
like little pieces of fluttering paper
they move fanatically against the screens:
let me in let me in.

But once in, they bang themselves against the curtain,
desperately looking for a way out.
Is this their life,
filled with extreme indecision and desperation?

The cats stare, no longer amused by their flight
no longer captivated by the movement of the small bodies
it may as well be a shadow to them.

Where are the butterflies?
Where are the small white butterflies?
I am grateful for the pink teacup roses and stamina of the tiger
lilies.
I am grateful for my fingers, hair, and body. The way my arms
spread and come back to me in the motion of a breaststroke.

In the garden people prepare their lawns.
Still the birds mingle with each other
and the grass sings its deep song.

Monarch Butterfly

He plants his careful kiss on my neck
and moves so slowly away.
I barely notice the wings moving
white and gold, with specks of purple and blue.
He is shy, careful not to cause a scene.

He is grace
and I am the sunset.
He is Amina
and I am lion.

He is the heather in the field of Rome,
and I am the water
with the small mosquito lodged above:
we are inevitable.

I am the Roman soldier who lost his last conflict.
The stone and the rose stand behind my shadow
like a tired wife, her aging shoulder against my rib.
My lost son sings me to sleep,
his armor an echo in my

heart.

Squirrel Weather

The verdant trees billow in the unseasonable
rain and wind of mid-May
bright marigolds bow their heads in semi-darkness

the grass reaches an apex of green
like the life of an adolescent squirrel
uncertain if he should leave the nest

wet green that calls to one in the dark morning

the new purple perennial
lavender and the white hydrangea
promise we will have another summer of deep love.

Rose

The roses that bloom in June are gone
in July. Fallen onto the ground.
My face the angle of a painting by Modigliani
gypsy with her baby
face muted, eyes the color of the sea,
small-mouthed,
neck long
like my mother's

in her first married home
she hung the painting in the living room
the scarf slightly turned against her swan neck;
                                    the baby close.

Still July

Thank God it is still July, when the bright underside of the leaf
outshines the topside.

The cats languish, perhaps they sweat
their whiskers protrude with some grave purpose
impossible for us to know.

The breeze plays off your shoulder and all the sadness you've ever
known
dies in the heat.

Come, friend, let's go to the same table and eat the same food
even though I do not know you.

The figs are almost in season,
but then it will be August.

Plant Life

I took my cat's hind legs and held them firm
their power
the soft padding where he jumps
high on the stockade fence.

Air seems to rise off the tops of the plants in August.
There is the buzzing of crickets in the thick green
and the dragonfly whirls.
Blue light shines off him—

undone, as we all are, by love.

Penstemon

Birds chirping echoes through the house
like madness or waves, a cacophony of wild screams.

The garden is overrun with stronger trees and plants
dominating the small roses and lilies.

They need a lesson in humility;
so do I.

I was lying in the hammock thinking of your hands on my body
and I heard a child say *I love you.*

In the grocery store I stop because
love has entered my heart
the morning glories take over the compost heap
and creep under the hostas
along the low grass.

The Virgin statue, newly painted, stands
with small white seashells at her feet,
yellow painted stars around her ankles.
It is a woman's garden
and the clematis stand tall
over the side wall like teenage girls
with long hair running and laughing in the sunlight;
no one can catch them.

Sheets

The wind blows the orange curtains in the room
they billow in the mid-August air
over the lilac-flowered sheets.

I am reminded of the ocean and how the waves pull
my whole body into redemption.
People are talking about how summer is ending;

have they no heart?

You came to me in a dream before I met you.
There were roses in the garden of small white rocks.
You told me things I never knew.

Was it Nietzsche who said that if you stare long enough into the
abyss, the abyss
gazes into you? What was he talking about? Echo and Narcissus?
*The shadow before six at night in the garden, or the light before the
morning?*

Tulip Tree

The purple salvia started up in the border garden today
along with the white and blue morning glories;
they occupy my mind.

On the hammock I face the tulip tree
somehow the small pink and red roses
started to rebloom.

I figure no one told them summer is ending.
Those small flowers just come up out of nowhere,
uninvited and adored.

Roman Garden

The light of August still exists in my fingertips and
in the four o'clock sun I saw a million gnats flying
yellow in the garden

I was released from suffering because
the sun glistened on their wings and suddenly a cat ran across
the driveway

like a dream.

Stalks of salvia wither and die
the morning glory wraps its small vines around the pussy willow,

to slowly say goodbye.

The Bed

I forgot the weight of your body
there is no wind to blow the white curtain.

I have forgotten your voice
the summer is ending.

Feast Day of the Assumption of the Blessed
Virgin Mary

Your eyes are shut next to mine
eyebrows, two brown tufted squares
freckled white skin even though it is August
hands curl under your face like my mother,
except when they lie across
the upper and lower half of your body
as if in conversation

about what, I cannot guess
a boy, perhaps, the way a girl holds her head,
a conversation you are not believing,
a certain striped top from Brandy Melville,
a silver turtle necklace; it is too hard to say
in this strong, silent dream nothing wakes you,
not even my movement from the bed.

In the car, arms crossed,
tennis shoes on the dashboard
there is not too much time
to convince you to take a sport, get your braces,
procure a tutor for math, to make everything all right.

Today the purple Delphinium has taken precedence
over the pink rosebush, temporarily and quietly withdrawing.
It is the larkspur I see every day as I draw the curtains.
At first, I thought it was a weed.
I let it stay, and it bloomed with no attention.
Tall, thin, small purple flowers, they open every day
and become more beautiful.

Emerald Year

Car Ride (Immaculate Conception)

On the Feast Day of the Immaculate Conception
I look at my daughter's face and realize that she is sixteen.
Her skin seems whiter
her nose straighter
she smiles less.

The small freckles on her chest
cluster together like a universe
spreading into an infinity like the iris of an eye
tiny green and brown stars shooting off from the origin
of darkness and subtle space
non-negotiable and irreversible.

Like a car riding up a mountainside,
you hear it in your ears before even recognizing the road

even the air is different.

Moment in the Sun

The cardinal sat high in the branch of the hackberry tree
basking his face in the sun
his crimson breast shone in the light like a soldier
in the 14th century
black jagged crown extending to heaven
small eyes glittering in the sun
believing in the end that it would be all right
believing as it were in the moment of the sun.

Witness 1

Witness the orange ochre leaves on the trees
right before they fall and end their life away from the tree.
How magnificent they are in all their color.

The solitary crow flies mildly in the sky

the mulberry bush turns from green to orange
fading into the endless red
fading into the heart
into the final light that will carry us through
winter's dusk days
the skunks will make their home
under the wild branches.

The tulip tree is green
and you think that will last forever
two days later the tree
in fullness is yellow.

Two crows sit contemplating the day on the green lawn.
One looks over his shoulder at me
as if to say, "What is it you want?
We're having a conversation here."

Witness 2

I feel like I'm 20, and I feel like I'm 60.
I feel like Clint Eastwood riding into the red-painted town
on his Appaloosa horse claiming to be not afraid
facing every possible danger
looking at the sun.

Has there been a brighter star than the unseen
under the slipper moon?

Today my heart is beating, and
my fingers move slow like one who is held back,
a moth feathered in loneliness.

Waiting for the Hurricane

Waiting for Hermine
waiting for my emerald year

to wake up.

The sea is flat before the storm.
The cats fight, but they don't mean it.

Until they do,
and this occurs when the older
one looks directly into the younger one's eyes
with his mouth ever so slightly open, and he lifts his paw up two
inches from the ground and makes an imperceptible sound and
breathes through his teeth
next to the bed, the small one stares, held in the trance of fear.

I was 11 my body lean and strong
the saltwater in my eyes, smiling at the thought of it all.

Love will come and shake the tree.
The leaves fall one by one
some green even, so soft to the ground
silent in the early day and then later
when the sky streaks with blue and black
and some kind of deliberate orange through the fall.

The hurricane is supposed to come today
in the middle of the sea
a circle of water
beneath which we will never know

the undercurrent of a life.

The cat's paw curls.

Skunks

It's high summer
skunks sleep under the porch.
After you left, I rinsed the sand off your flip-flops
and put them on the picnic table.

I held your hand in the car;
it was like holding a bird.
I felt the fluttering heartbeat of your small, thin fingers.
Suddenly it occurred to me: this fragility.

Only once did the family of skunks venture out together.
They seemed resigned to stand near the side garden in the dusk,
observing what was available.
One of them discovered the bird bath and languished in the water

twirling his white body
with the black single stripe.
He was a child
of God.

Nantasket

Halved mussel shells scatter the shoreline
the blue within the black
the seagulls have gone quiet
piping plovers lift their bodies
over the crest of waves and the small
black feet hang like questions
above the water.
After years of doubt,
we are learning to live

with the waves.

About the Author

Gloria Monaghan is a professor of Humanities at Wentworth Institute in Boston. She has published four books of poetry: *Flawed* (Finishing Line Press, 2011, nominated for the Massachusetts Book Award), *The Garden* (Flutter Press, 2015), *False Spring* (Adelaide Books, 2019), and *Torero* (Nixes Mate, 2020). Her poems have appeared in *Blue Max Review, 2River, Adelaide, the Aurorean,* and *First Literary Review-East,* among others. In 2018, her poem "Into Grace" was nominated for a Pushcart Prize.